KINDERGARTEN VOCABULARY

Fun-filled Activities

An imprint of Om Books International

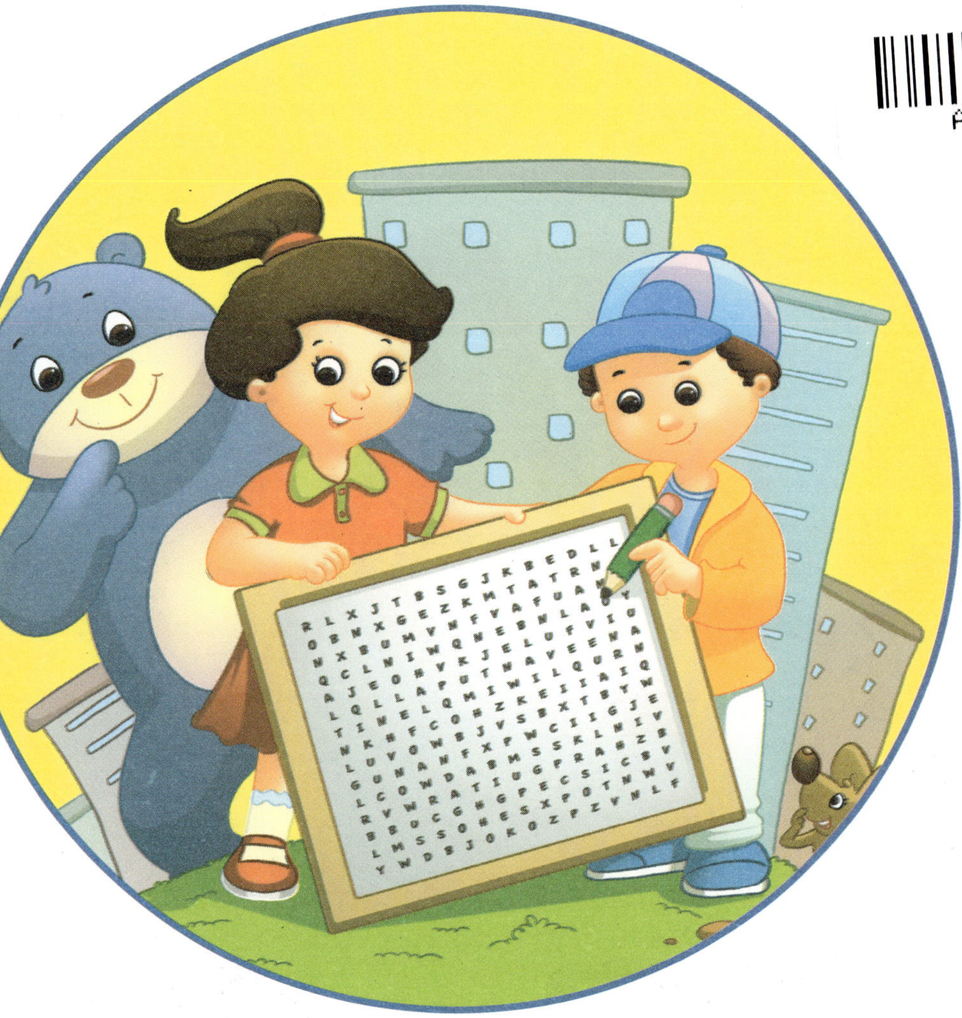

Short a Sound As In Cap

Say aloud the name of each picture given below. Circle (O) the pictures that have the sound of short a as in cap.

A

Short a Sound

Look at all the pictures given below and match them with their names.

Short a Sound

The letters have all changed their positions. Write the correct short **a** words for the pictures.

a p n

______

______

a t g

______

______

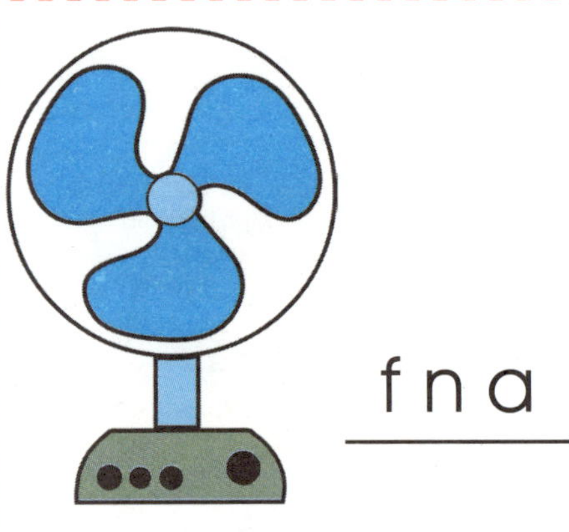

f n a

______

______

a t n

______

______

m n a

______

______

k c s a

______

______

c p l a

______

______

f a l g

______

______

Long a Sound As In Nail

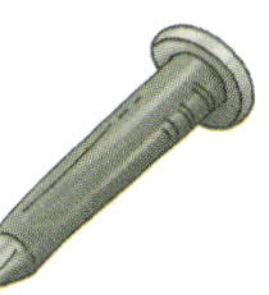

Name each picture. Circle (O) those with the long a sound.

Long a Sound

Read each word below. Then find them in the word search.

made	rate	cake	game	late
race	lake	grape	gate	lace

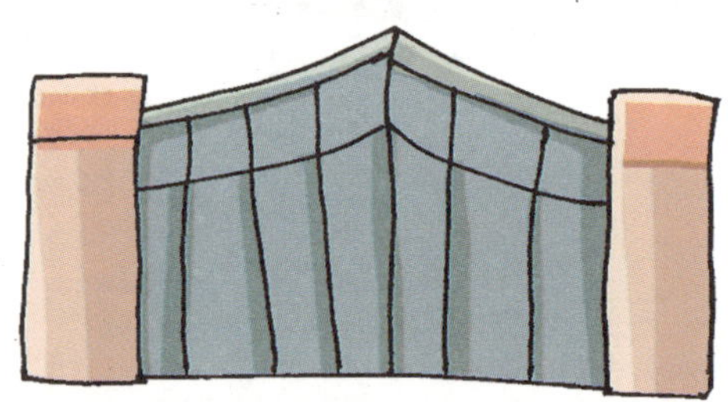

z	g	a	m	e	c	a	k	e
r	a	t	e	y	u	g	s	h
a	p	e	i	f	d	r	a	m
c	w	a	s	t	e	a	s	a
e	o	d	b	l	e	p	t	d
p	g	s	n	a	k	e	a	e
l	f	p	a	c	i	p	t	b
a	r	a	k	e	a	d	e	m
t	a	c	g	z	n	e	p	l
e	m	e	a	n	a	m	e	a
a	e	t	v	l	a	t	e	k
t	a	m	e	n	g	a	t	e

Long a Sound

Say the name of each picture. Colour the correct letters and write the word.

Picture	Colour	write
	v a s c w t o e	vase
	a c p o w m i e	
	c m a o j i g e	
	p l q a v o t e	
	t y r a e o i n	

Short e Sound As In Red

Roll the dice. Read and check-off short e words in each column according to the number on the dice as shown below.

☑ pen	☐ tan	☐ men
☐ wag	☐ bell	☐ let
☐ nest	☐ ant	☐ can
☐ lad	☐ belt	☐ elk
☐ vest	☐ desk	☐ sled
☐ leg	☐ yak	☐ van
⚀ or ⚁	⚂ or ⚃	⚄ or ⚅

Short e Sound

Fill in the crossword with short e words. Take help of the word bank.

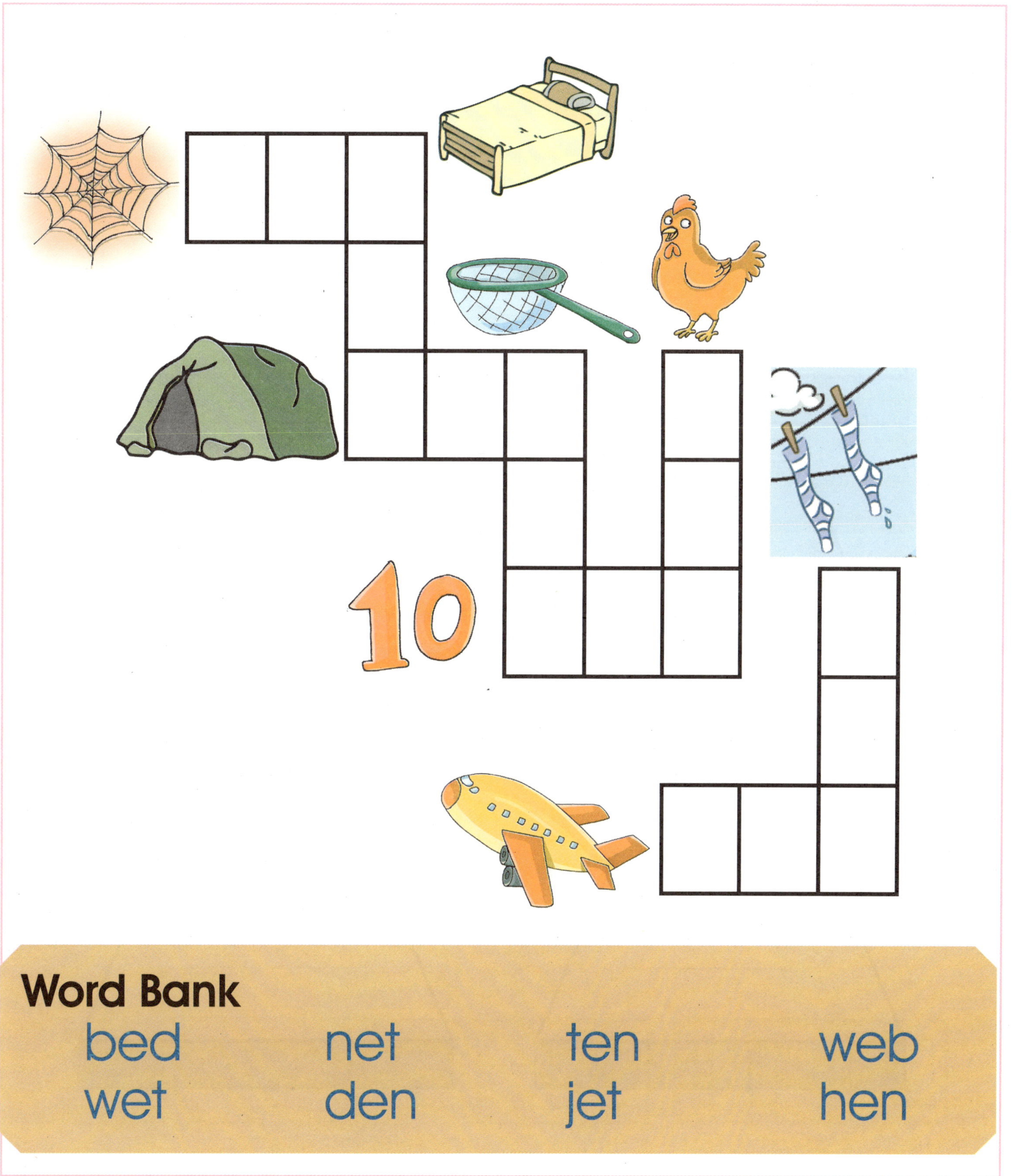

Word Bank

bed	net	ten	web
wet	den	jet	hen

Short e Sound

Look at the first word in each shape. Change the first letter and make new short e words. Use the letters in the boxes.

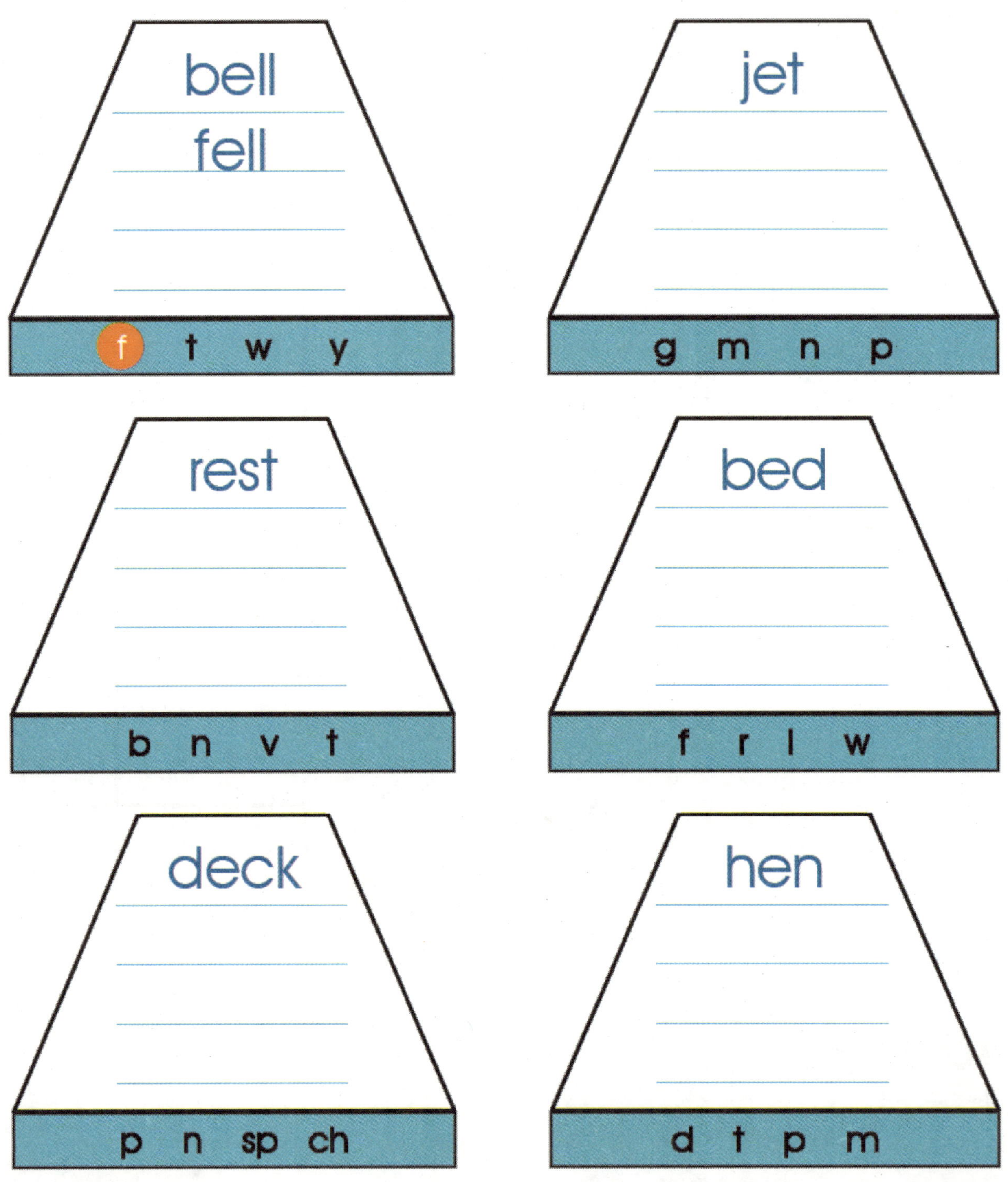

Long e Sound As In Bee

Say the name of each picture in the rows below. Circle (O) the pictures whose names have a long **e** sound.

Long e Sound

Use a paper clip and pencil to spin the spinner. Write the letters on the blanks. If it is a long **e** word, circle it.

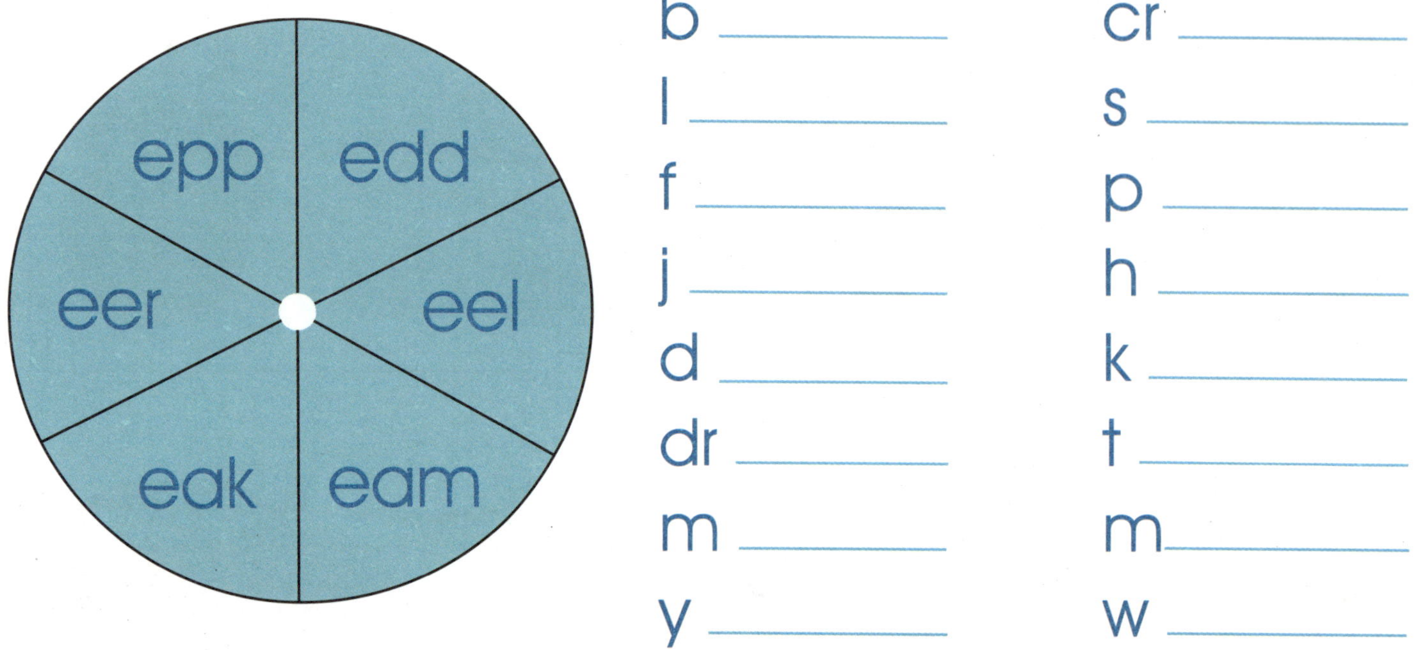

Name and colour the picture. Draw a shell if the name has a long **e** sound.

Long e Sound

Use the picture clues and complete the crossword with long **e** words. Then write the words in the blanks.

1.

2.

3.

4.

5.

6.

7.

8.

9.

10.

Short i Sound As In Bin 

Say aloud the name of each picture. Circle (O) the ones that have the short i sound.

Short i Sound

Say the name of each picture. Write the letter i to complete the words.

w g

m lk

r ng

g ft

Short i Sound

Look at the picture codes and pick the letters. Complete the words with a short i sound.

b, f, s, h	b, d, f, p	t, p, ch, sp	w, st, gr, fr	s, cl, wh, sk	i, th, pr, tr

-it	-ig	-in	-ill	-ip	-ick

Long i Sound As In Kite

Match the pictures with the correct words.

smile

five

hive

lime

fire

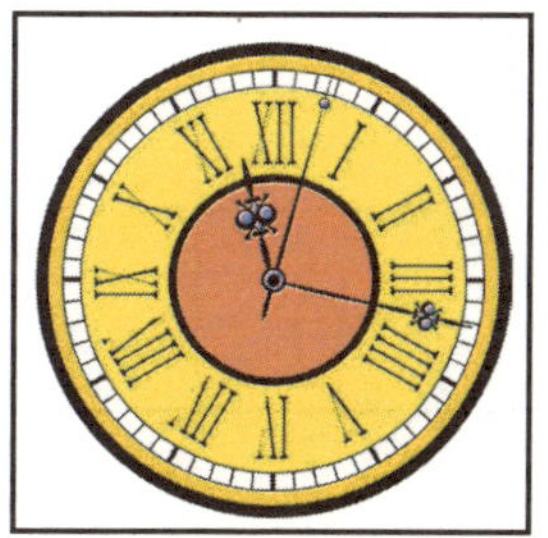

dice

vine

time

Long i Sound

Look and circle (O) the words with the long i sound in the puzzle.

k	h	r	d	e	d	t	i	l	e	f	s
i	k	l	i	g	h	t	g	d	m	b	t
t	s	y	e	s	i	t	o	p	s	g	i
e	h	s	i	e	g	r	l	s	e	p	e
y	f	i	n	e	h	l	i	k	e	n	p
e	a	p	e	n	h	e	e	r	d	b	i
a	t	c	f	i	n	d	b	g	m	g	c
r	i	l	r	d	k	a	y	i	d	n	n
p	r	i	b	i	k	e	s	e	s	m	i
w	e	r	k	p	e	n	i	d	i	a	g
p	a	c	e	n	i	g	h	t	g	p	h
r	i	d	e	y	a	r	e	a	n	z	t

- kite
- bike
- tie
- light
- fine

- ride
- tire
- tile
- night
- lie

- find
- die
- like
- sign
- high

Long i Sound

Circle (O) all the words with a long i sound.

cry	fight	pine
hot	three	line
fly	mine	high
bite	frog	tiger

Write the long i words you found.

Draw

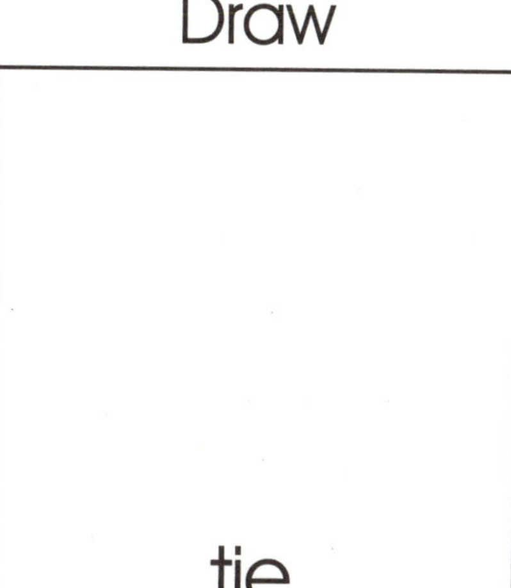

tie

ice

Fill in the missing letters.

l		g	h	

Short o Sound As In Top

Draw a line from o to the pictures whose names have a short o sound.

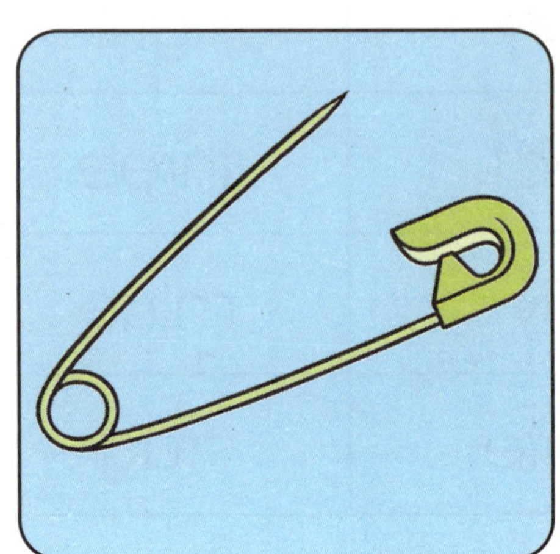

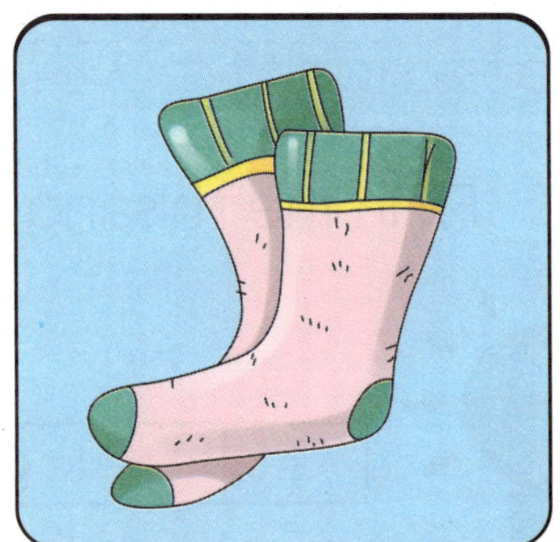

Short o Sound

Say the name of each picture below. Circle (O) the pictures with the short o sound.

Circle (O) the words with the short o sound.

cold	top	son	go
jog	old	hot	lot
not	fog	over	cop

How does a rabbit move? Write the word.

Long o Sound As In Bone 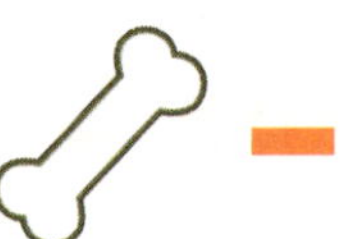

Write names of the pictures that have a long o sound.

Long o Sound

Say the name of each picture below. Connect the pictures with the letter o in the centre.

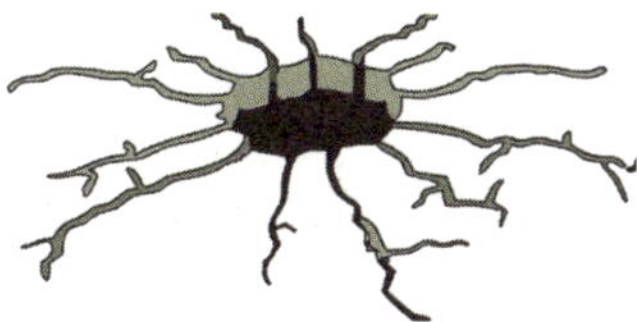

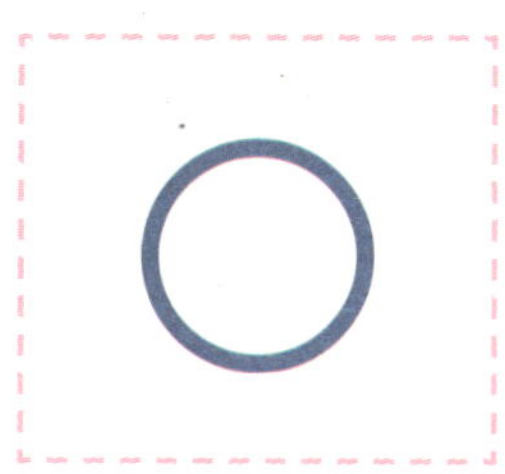

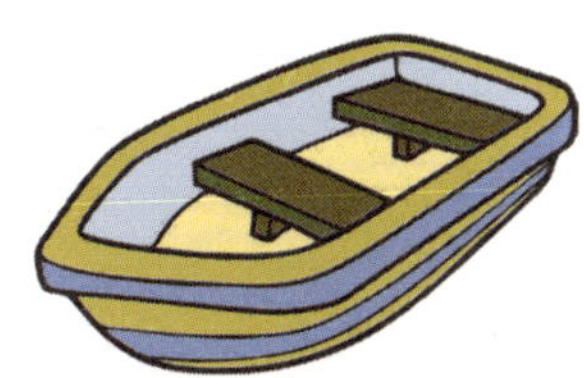

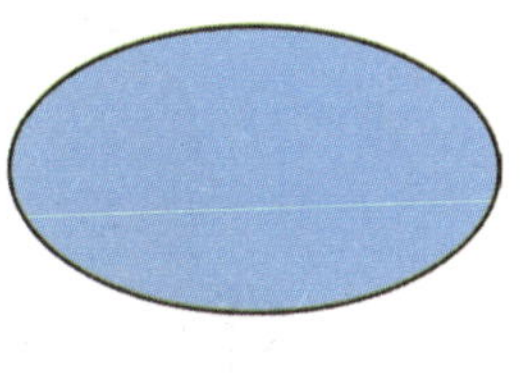

Circle (O) the words with a long o sound.

cold	top
son	snow
over	old
cop	fog
jag	go
both	close

Draw a picture of something that has long o sound in its name.

Write a word with the long o sound.

Long o Sound

Match the pictures with the words by writing the correct numbers.

1. hose	2. nose	3. globe
4. coal	5. goat	6. loaf
7. crow	8. smoke	9. robe

Short u Sound As In Cup

Colour the balloons with short u words.

top
rug
gut
but
fun
cup
pup
gap
tuck
dug
sun

Short u Sound

Put a tick (✓) on pictures whose names have the short u sound.

Short u Sound

Use the word families to make short u words.

ud	ug	up	uck	un	ub	um	ut

1. b______
2. h______
3. c______
4. s______
5. p______
6. r______
7. b______
8. t______
9. c______
10. c______
11. h______
12. b______
13. d______
14. s______
15. p______
16. c______
17. r______
18. n______
19. b______
20. s______
21. m______
22. j______
23. c______
24. h______

Long u Sound As In Cube 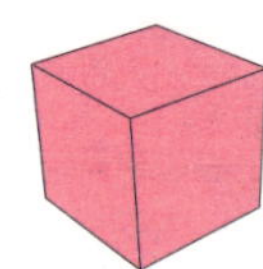

Circle (O) the pictures whose names have a long **u** sound.

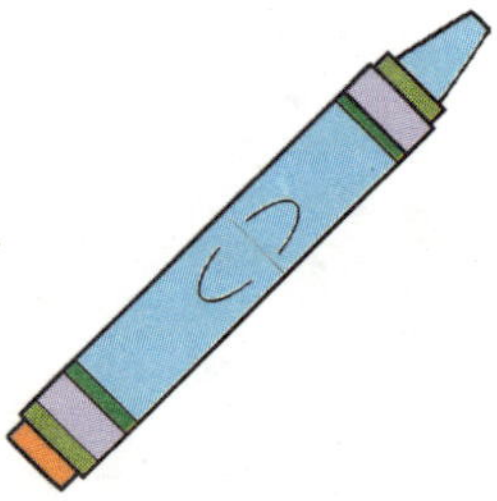

Long u Sound

Use the letter clues on the right and fill in the blanks.

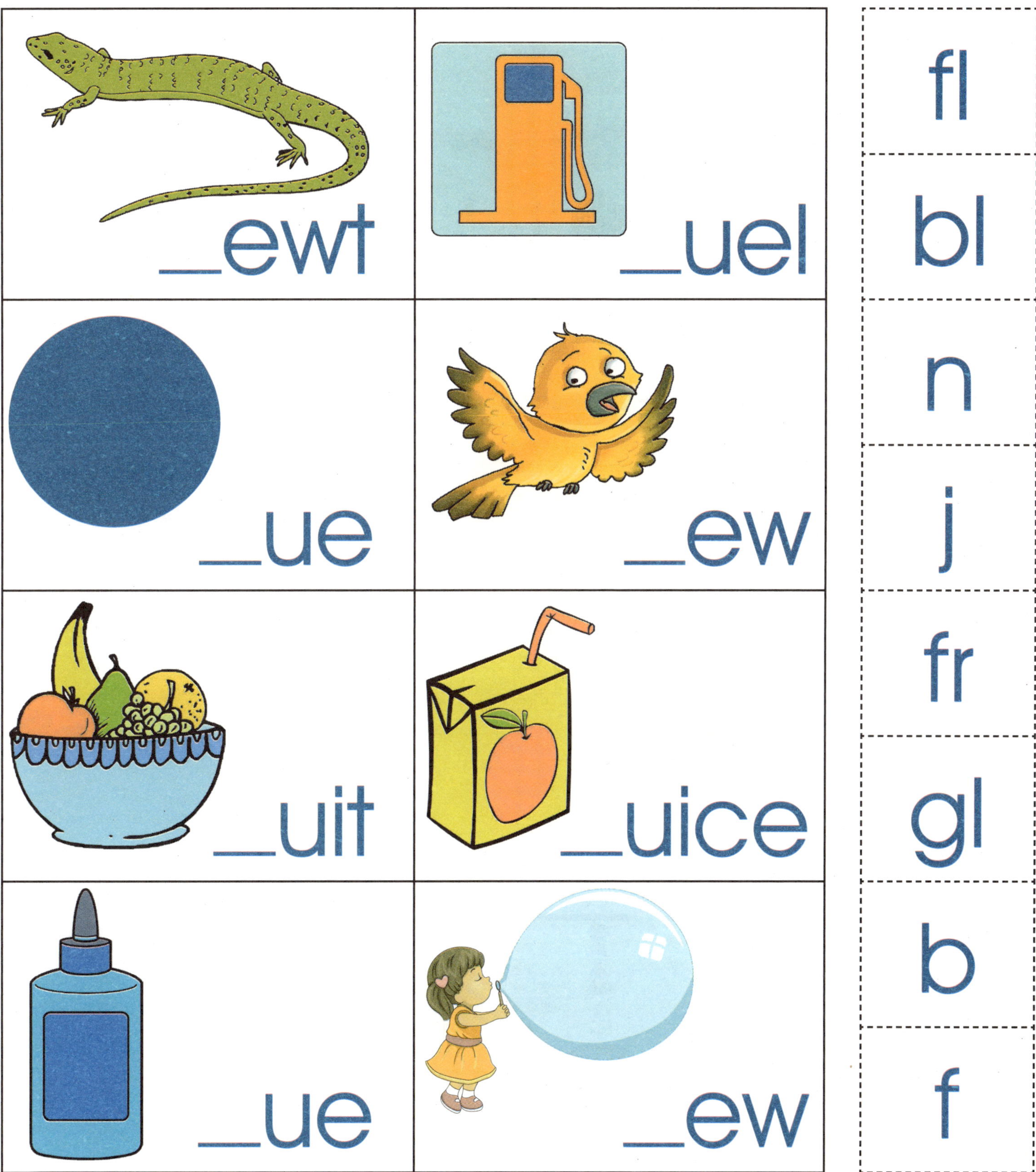

Answer Key

Page 2

Page 5

Page 8

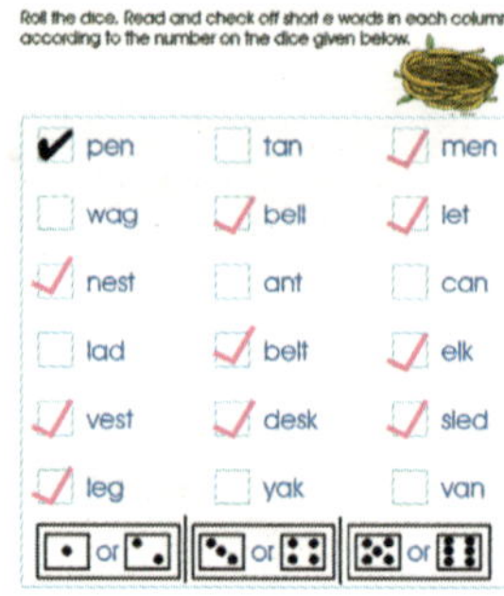

Page 3

Page 6

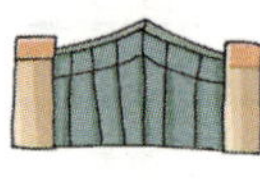

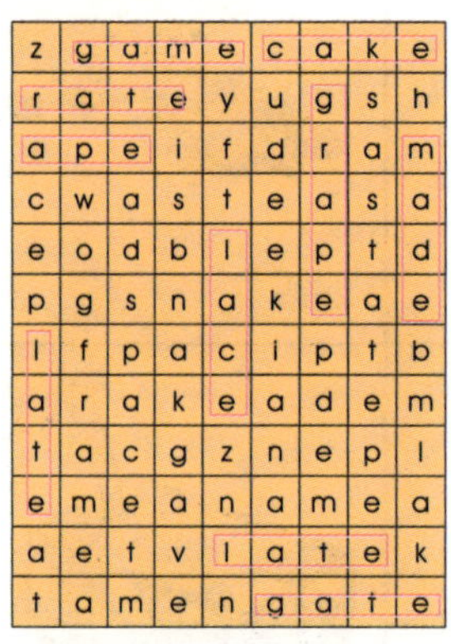

Page 9

Page 4

Page 7

Page 10

Children to do on their own

Answer Key

Page 11

Page 12

Children to do on their own

Page 13

Across:	Down :
2. Leaf	1. Eat
3. Seed	3. Sleep
5. Tea	4. Read
6. Three	5. Turkey
7. Monkey	8. Net

Page 14

Page 15

Children to do on their own

Page 16

Children to do on their own

Page 17

Page 18

Look and circle the words with the long i sound in the puzzle.

k	h	r	d	e	d	t	i	l	e	f	s
i	k	l	i	g	h	t	g	d	m	b	t
t	s	y	e	s	i	t	o	p	s	g	i
e	h	s	i	e	g	r	l	s	e	p	e
y	f	i	n	e	h	l	i	k	e	n	p
e	a	p	e	n	h	e	e	r	d	b	i
a	t	c	f	i	n	d	b	g	m	g	c
r	i	l	r	d	k	a	y	i	d	n	n
p	r	i	b	i	k	e	s	e	s	m	i
w	e	r	k	p	e	n	i	d	i	a	g
p	a	c	e	n	i	g	h	t	g	p	h
r	i	d	e	y	a	r	e	a	n	z	t

- kite
- bike
- tie
- light
- fine
- ride
- tire
- tile
- night
- lie
- find
- die
- like
- sign
- high

Page 19

Words are:

fight, pine, line, mine, high, bite, tiger, light

Page 20

Answer Key

Page 21

Page 22

Children will do on their own

Page 23

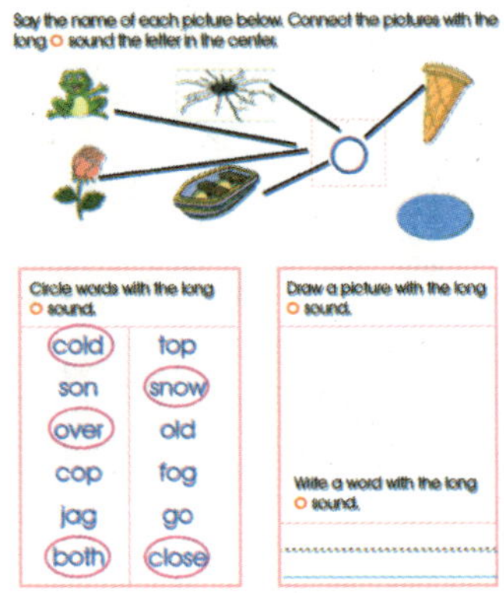

Page 24

Write these numbers on the pictures:

3- globe, 2- nose, 4- coal

1- hose, 8- smoke, 7- crow

5- goat , 6- loaf 9- robe

Page 25

Children to do on their own

Page 26

Page 27

Children to do on their own

Page 28

Page 29

The words are:

newt, fuel, blue, flew, fruit, juice, glue, blew